I0402822

The Multidimensional Profits Prism

An Entrepreneur's Creation Planner For Designing Multidimensional Profits Models

AliNICOLE "WATERS"

The Multidimensional Profits Prism

ISBN-9781690027195

Printed in the United States of America by Kindle Direct Publishing

The Multidimensional Profits Prism

How To See Your Entrepreneurship In Different Dimensions & Create Your Profitable Multidimensional Empire

Imagine yourself to be a prism with many facets that light can shine through. With each aspect or side of the prism, there are different dimensions that each have great significance. As you see the light shine through the prism you often see the rainbow colors reflected.

As it relates to your brand and business in a new era marketplace, you want to make sure that you're demonstrating diversity and multiplicity to showcase different variations of your uniqueness. Having a prism effect allows you to showcase yourself and offerings in several ways.

The different dimensions of your brand and business represent the "Profit Portals" that can catapult you into realms of infinite possibilities. These "Profit Portals" introduce you to the basics of your Multidimensional Profits Prism. One of my dear friends, divine-soul sister, and colleague, Rene Johnson once described me as a prism that reflected all of the various dimensions of colors because of how I show up in conscious multiplicity to make an impact and income.

I love prisms and no one had ever described me as one so her powerful words inspired me to rename this work from The Multidimensional Profits Factor to the Multidimensional Profits Prism.

The Multidimensional Profits Prism

Your multidimensional profits prism reflects your higher creation potential for developing your best products, services, and profits agenda. I would like for you to picture yourself, your brand, and your business like Matryoshka dolls that have several dolls within one doll.

There are different dimensions of your potential, brilliance, and branding. Just when you think you've seen the greatest expansion for your mission or vision, you'll discover that there's so much more that desires to come forth.

So often the very reason why there's a limitation to the impact and income that most entrepreneurs make is that they level out too soon by getting stuck in a one niche wonder framework, solely focused on marketing one or two core offers and don't allow other aspects of their brand or business to breakthrough for a greater purpose, possibilities, and profits.

It's time to start seeing your brand, products and services beyond just a one-dimensional vantage point. Your profits model is multi-layered and should consist of at least three to five different profits agendas that can each be expressed as a standalone empire if necessary.

I created the platform Multidimensional Profits Models to help new era entrepreneurs take the limits off of how they make their impact and income by seeing the different dimensions of potential and possibility. I realize that not everyone can work with me so my intention was to provide this creation planner to help others set new profits intentions, become aware of their multidimensional profits prism effect, and design a new empire framework for success in a self-paced fashion.

The Multidimensional Profits Prism

This process involves continuously asking empowering questions, seeing your brand, business and offerings through expanded visioning, and developing master profits planning at a higher level.

Use this creation planner section to reflect and record your insights from the reading, brainstorming, and more. Treat your empire and profits agenda like your business partner and take time to get present with the series of questions that are provided. These questions will help you to create your multidimensional profits model with ease and design a new profits prism for your next levels of success.

The Multidimensional Profits Prism

The Multidimensional Profits Portal Creation Planner Section

New Colors, New Dimensions
New Value, New Profits

Ask your product, service, or profits model...

Are you single or multidimensional in nature?

How many different levels desire to be expressed at this time?

The Multidimensional Profits Prism

Are you in your final form for this phase?

How can I make these offerings more valuable?

The Multidimensional Profits Prism

What is my current multidimensional profits prism factor?

What are the best ways to create a solid profit plan for my multidimensional empire at this phase?

The Multidimensional Profits Prism

Creation Planning

Design a new profits prism model or plan using the insights and wisdom gained from your answers to the questions.

More Notes

New Colors, New Dimensions
New Value, New Profits

Ask your product, service, or profits model...

Are you single or multidimensional in nature?

How many different levels desire to be expressed at this time?

The Multidimensional Profits Prism

Are you in your final form for this phase?

How can I make these offerings more valuable?

The Multidimensional Profits Prism

What is my current multidimensional profits prism factor?

What are the best ways to create a solid profit plan for my multidimensional empire at this phase?

The Multidimensional Profits Prism

Creation Planning

Design a new profits prism model or plan using the insights and wisdom gained from your answers to the questions.

The Multidimensional Profits Prism

More Notes

New Colors, New Dimensions
New Value, New Profits

Ask your product, service, or profits model...

Are you single or multidimensional in nature?

How many different levels desire to be expressed at this time?

The Multidimensional Profits Prism

Are you in your final form for this phase?

How can I make these offerings more valuable?

The Multidimensional Profits Prism

What is my current multidimensional profits prism factor?

What are the best ways to create a solid profit plan for my multidimensional empire at this phase?

Creation Planning

Design a new profits prism model or plan using the insights and wisdom gained from your answers to the questions.

More Notes

The Multidimensional Profits Prism

New Colors, New Dimensions
New Value, New Profits

Ask your product, service, or profits model...

Are you single or multidimensional in nature?

How many different levels desire to be expressed at this time?

The Multidimensional Profits Prism

Are you in your final form for this phase?

How can I make these offerings more valuable?

The Multidimensional Profits Prism

What is my current multidimensional profits prism factor?

What are the best ways to create a solid profit plan for my multidimensional empire at this phase?

The Multidimensional Profits Prism

Creation Planning

Design a new profits prism model or plan using the insights and wisdom gained from your answers to the questions.

The Multidimensional Profits Prism

More Notes

New Colors, New Dimensions
New Value, New Profits

Ask your product, service, or profits model...

Are you single or multidimensional in nature?

How many different levels desire to be expressed at this time?

The Multidimensional Profits Prism

Are you in your final form for this phase?

How can I make these offerings more valuable?

The Multidimensional Profits Prism

What is my current multidimensional profits prism factor?

What are the best ways to create a solid profit plan for my multidimensional empire at this phase?

Creation Planning

Design a new profits prism model or plan using the insights and wisdom gained from your answers to the questions.

More Notes

New Colors, New Dimensions
New Value, New Profits

Ask your product, service, or profits model...

Are you single or multidimensional in nature?

How many different levels desire to be expressed at this time?

The Multidimensional Profits Prism

Are you in your final form for this phase?

How can I make these offerings more valuable?

The Multidimensional Profits Prism

What is my current multidimensional profits prism factor?

What are the best ways to create a solid profit plan for my multidimensional empire at this phase?

The Multidimensional Profits Prism

Creation Planning

Design a new profits prism model or plan using the insights and wisdom gained from your answers to the questions.

The Multidimensional Profits Prism

More Notes

New Colors, New Dimensions
New Value, New Profits

Ask your product, service, or profits model...

Are you single or multidimensional in nature?

How many different levels desire to be expressed at this time?

The Multidimensional Profits Prism

Are you in your final form for this phase?

How can I make these offerings more valuable?

The Multidimensional Profits Prism

New Colors, New Dimensions
New Value, New Profits

Ask your product, service, or profits model...

Are you single or multidimensional in nature?

How many different levels desire to be expressed at this time?

The Multidimensional Profits Prism

Are you in your final form for this phase?

How can I make these offerings more valuable?

The Multidimensional Profits Prism

What is my current multidimensional profits prism factor?

What are the best ways to create a solid profit plan for my multidimensional empire at this phase?

Creation Planning

Design a new profits prism model or plan using the insights and wisdom gained from your answers to the questions.

More Notes

New Colors, New Dimensions
New Value, New Profits

Ask your product, service, or profits model...

Are you single or multidimensional in nature?

How many different levels desire to be expressed at this time?

The Multidimensional Profits Prism

Are you in your final form for this phase?

How can I make these offerings more valuable?

The Multidimensional Profits Prism

What is my current multidimensional profits prism factor?

What are the best ways to create a solid profit plan for my multidimensional empire at this phase?

Creation Planning

Design a new profits prism model or plan using the insights and wisdom gained from your answers to the questions.

The Multidimensional Profits Prism

More Notes

New Colors, New Dimensions
New Value, New Profits

Ask your product, service, or profits model...

Are you single or multidimensional in nature?

How many different levels desire to be expressed at this time?

The Multidimensional Profits Prism

Are you in your final form for this phase?

How can I make these offerings more valuable?

The Multidimensional Profits Prism

What is my current multidimensional profits prism factor?

What are the best ways to create a solid profit plan for my multidimensional empire at this phase?

The Multidimensional Profits Prism

Creation Planning

Design a new profits prism model or plan using the insights and wisdom gained from your answers to the questions.

More Notes

New Colors, New Dimensions
New Value, New Profits

Ask your product, service, or profits model...

Are you single or multidimensional in nature?

How many different levels desire to be expressed at this time?

The Multidimensional Profits Prism

More Notes

New Colors, New Dimensions
New Value, New Profits

Ask your product, service, or profits model...

Are you single or multidimensional in nature?

How many different levels desire to be expressed at this time?

The Multidimensional Profits Prism

Are you in your final form for this phase?

How can I make these offerings more valuable?

The Multidimensional Profits Prism

What is my current multidimensional profits prism factor?

What are the best ways to create a solid profit plan for my multidimensional empire at this phase?

The Multidimensional Profits Prism

Creation Planning

Design a new profits prism model or plan using the insights and wisdom gained from your answers to the questions.

The Multidimensional Profits Prism

More Notes

The Multidimensional Profits Prism

New Colors, New Dimensions
New Value, New Profits

Ask your product, service, or profits model...

Are you single or multidimensional in nature?

How many different levels desire to be expressed at this time?

The Multidimensional Profits Prism

Are you in your final form for this phase?

How can I make these offerings more valuable?

The Multidimensional Profits Prism

What is my current multidimensional profits prism factor?

What are the best ways to create a solid profit plan for my multidimensional empire at this phase?

Creation Planning

Design a new profits prism model or plan using the insights and wisdom gained from your answers to the questions.

More Notes

The Multidimensional Profits Prism

New Colors, New Dimensions
New Value, New Profits

Ask your product, service, or profits model...

Are you single or multidimensional in nature?

How many different levels desire to be expressed at this time?

The Multidimensional Profits Prism

Are you in your final form for this phase?

How can I make these offerings more valuable?

The Multidimensional Profits Prism

What is my current multidimensional profits prism factor?

What are the best ways to create a solid profit plan for my multidimensional empire at this phase?

Creation Planning

Design a new profits prism model or plan using the insights and wisdom gained from your answers to the questions.

The Multidimensional Profits Prism

More Notes

The Multidimensional Profits Prism

New Colors, New Dimensions
New Value, New Profits

Ask your product, service, or profits model...

Are you single or multidimensional in nature?

How many different levels desire to be expressed at this time?

The Multidimensional Profits Prism

Are you in your final form for this phase?

How can I make these offerings more valuable?

The Multidimensional Profits Prism

What is my current multidimensional profits prism factor?

What are the best ways to create a solid profit plan for my multidimensional empire at this phase?

The Multidimensional Profits Prism

Creation Planning

Design a new profits prism model or plan using the insights and wisdom gained from your answers to the questions.

More Notes

The Multidimensional Profits Prism

New Colors, New Dimensions
New Value, New Profits

Ask your product, service, or profits model...

Are you single or multidimensional in nature?

How many different levels desire to be expressed at this time?

The Multidimensional Profits Prism

Are you in your final form for this phase?

How can I make these offerings more valuable?

The Multidimensional Profits Prism

What is my current multidimensional profits prism factor?

What are the best ways to create a solid profit plan for my multidimensional empire at this phase?

The Multidimensional Profits Prism

Creation Planning

Design a new profits prism model or plan using the insights and wisdom gained from your answers to the questions.

More Notes

New Colors, New Dimensions
New Value, New Profits

Ask your product, service, or profits model...

Are you single or multidimensional in nature?

How many different levels desire to be expressed at this time?

The Multidimensional Profits Prism

Are you in your final form for this phase?

How can I make these offerings more valuable?

The Multidimensional Profits Prism

What is my current multidimensional profits prism factor?

What are the best ways to create a solid profit plan for my multidimensional empire at this phase?

The Multidimensional Profits Prism

Creation Planning

Design a new profits prism model or plan using the insights and wisdom gained from your answers to the questions.

More Notes

The Multidimensional Profits Prism

New Colors, New Dimensions
New Value, New Profits

Ask your product, service, or profits model...

Are you single or multidimensional in nature?

How many different levels desire to be expressed at this time?

The Multidimensional Profits Prism

Are you in your final form for this phase?

How can I make these offerings more valuable?

The Multidimensional Profits Prism

What is my current multidimensional profits prism factor?

What are the best ways to create a solid profit plan for my multidimensional empire at this phase?

The Multidimensional Profits Prism

Creation Planning

Design a new profits prism model or plan using the insights and wisdom gained from your answers to the questions.

The Multidimensional Profits Prism

More Notes

The Multidimensional Profits Prism

For More Related Resources
Visit:
www.multidimensionalprofitsmodels.tumblr.com

Visit Author's Page for More
Resources for Different Industries
www.amazon.com/author/alicianwaters

To Book Author for Speaking Engagements

Email: anwempires@gmail.com

If you enjoyed this resource, please
consider writing a review on Amazon.com.

Thanks & Blessings!

The Multidimensional Profits Prism

www.ingramcontent.com/pod-product-compliance
Lightning Source LLC
Chambersburg PA
CBHW070811220526

45466CB00002B/640